Welcome to the Magic of Christmas!

Thank you for choosing this coloring book dedicated to the magic of Christmas. Each page is designed to capture the festive spirit, with illustrations that evoke warmth, joy, and serenity.

These pages were created to offer you a moment of relaxation, a peaceful break amidst the holiday hustle and bustle.

While Amazon's paper works well with colored pencils and alcohol-based markers, if you're using watercolors or other wet mediums, always place a thicker sheet of paper behind the page you're coloring to prevent smudging."

CUTE CHRISTMAS
COLORING BOOK
Tessa J Amelle

Made in the USA
Las Vegas, NV
02 November 2024

11005687R10037